156 Ways to Market Your Local Business

*and **stand out** from your competition*

Nick Williams

First published in Great Britain in 2019 by Nick Williams

ISBN: 978-1-944066-23-9

Head on over to our Facebook page:

https://www.facebook.com/LocalBusinessMarketingIdeas

to connect with other amazing local business owners around
the World.

Creations
Local Business Marketing

www.creations.marketing

Contents

Acknowledgments

I'd like to thank all the amazing business owners that have kindly allowed me to include examples of their great work within this book. You are an inspiration to us all.

I'd like to thank everyone that has kindly provided a testimonial for the book. Your constructive feedback has been a big help throughout this whole process.

Finally, I'd like to say a huge thank you to all our clients. I love waking up every day and working with you towards your dreams. They say that when you love what you do it shouldn't feel like work and I can honestly say that is the case working alongside you. Some of you have already gone through huge transformations in your business and I want to thank you for believing in me to help you achieve your dream.

This book is dedicated to my wife, my children, and my parents. Without your help, encouragement, and love, this book wouldn't have been possible.

Foreword

Mention the word 'marketing' to many small business owners and you can see them visibly shudder at the mere thought of it. Whilst many appreciate the necessity of it, often they lack enthusiasm and certainly the time to be able to put together a whole strategy that will work to support their business. *What does it really mean? What do I have to do?* And, *how much will it cost me in time and money?* Are just some of the questions they come up with.

Enter Nick Williams. I met Nick just a few months ago and was immediately enthused by his great ambition to dispel the myths about marketing. Nick has the ability to inspire everyone to do and be more, and for those of us who struggle for time, then Nick even has the solution – he can do it for you!

So, who better to write a book on the subject than Nick? And what a great book it is. The key concepts and ideas that Nick shares here are well worth reading. Even if you are a seasoned marketer, there will certainly be an idea or two to spark a new campaign or initiative in your business. Take notes and take action. Good Luck!

Tricia Wellings
Director & Founder Foundation Focus & MBK Training

Introduction

First of all, I just want to congratulate you on being brave enough to open your own business. You are helping to make a huge contribution to the economy and are providing families with a living whilst still giving customers the opportunity to buy your products and services locally. Along with that, you are also dealing with all the stresses and strains that running your own business can bring. So again, I just want to congratulate you and tell you well done for doing such a great job. Small business owners need to be given far more credit for their contributions.

It's hard running any business, particularly a service-based, bricks and mortar business, when a huge amount of your time is taken up with dealing with customers face to face and having more overheads, in comparison to a business that is purely online.

There are five core areas to a business:

Marketing, sales, operations, delivery and finance. Typically, most business owners are good at the operations and delivery. With all your other priorities, marketing can often be neglected; but a new customer could be worth a huge amount to your business. Often we spend hardly any time marketing our services to those prospects to get them to buy in the first place and then neglect to build on that relationship when they do become a customer. But building a relationship with your customer is vital to success. It's what I call 'customer relationship marketing'. So, what does that mean? Well, it's not just about marketing your business to get in a new enquiry, it's then continuing to market and nurture your relationship when they are a customer, so you encourage them to buy more from you and refer others to do the same.

I wrote this book to share ideas that my wife and I have implemented in our businesses and with our clients in the hope that it will encourage you to do the same. The majority of the concepts in here are easy to implement and can be done very quickly. You can either read this book page by page or jump to a section that you've already started work on. This book isn't a guarantee of success though; nothing will happen unless you implement these concepts fully into your business and make marketing a key priority for your growth and success.

The concepts within this book are the key to supercharging your marketing efforts in a very short period of time, but nothing can ever replace a network of peer group support and accountability. That's why you should head to www.creations.marketing and continue your journey with us directly. You'll discover lots of free content, resources, podcasts, and the opportunity to grow faster with our coaching and mentorship programs.

We hope you enjoy the book.

Fundamentals

Introduction

Before we get into the core tactics within the book, I just wanted to cover some fundamentals that I wish I had put in place when I started my first business. These fundamentals will help you create a solid foundation to start your marketing, so I'd highly recommend putting them in place before you start to spend any money on marketing your business.

Know your ideal customers (your customer avatar)

I'm not just talking about being general here. You need to define the gender, age bracket, background, job, likes and dislikes of your ideal customer, as well as identifying why they would come to you over another business. Once you know your ideal customer, you can market to them accordingly. You'll probably find that when you do this task you'll end up having more than one type of customer. That's fine, providing you then market to them accordingly.

Once you have all the information we've outlined above you can then start to create a story of that customer.

Here's an example of an ideal customer for a childcare business:

Mary is 32 with 3 children aged 6, 3, and 1. She loves her children dearly, but is also very career driven and Dad is away a lot, so she doesn't get a lot of support. Mary requires care 4 days a week and then has Friday at home to collect the children and spend time with her youngest two children. Mary chose our nursery because she loves the family approach and the location was perfect. She loves daily progress from her children's key workers and appreciates the gifts that we send out to her for birthdays. She always joins in our posts on Facebook and always enters competitions.

Elevator pitch

Imagine if you entered a lift with your perfect ideal customer. You've got 15 seconds before they get out of the lift to explain what you do and why they should come to you.

So, here is a template you could use to create your own elevator pitch:

My name is [insert name]. I help [business / people] to / with [insert problem] by providing them with [insert solution]. [Call to action].

My name is Nick Williams. I help local business owners to generate more customers quickly and automate their marketing by providing them with access to our proprietary C5 Marketing System. If you'd like to give me your email I can send out a link for you to see exactly what I could do for your business.

Solve their problems

People are usually looking for a solution to a problem and those problems usually fall into one of three categories:

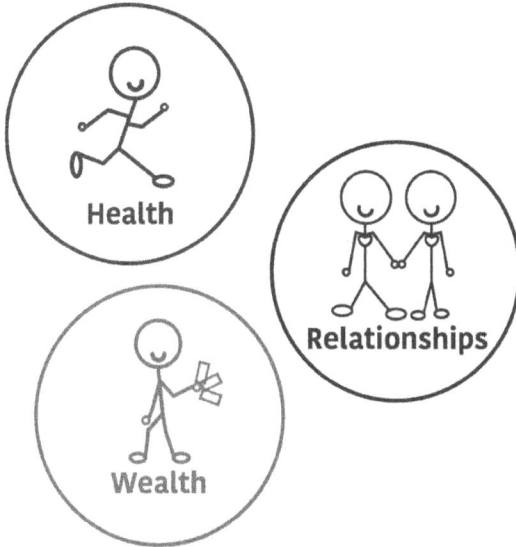

Here are some examples:

- When Gillette are promoting their brand-new razor online, the advert usually ends with the guy getting the girl. So, they are technically promoting relationships.

- The local spa maybe promoting a new anti-aging treatment. So technically they could be promoting health or relationships.

Whilst your product or service might not fit directly into one of these three categories, it is important that your marketing message does fit into one of these three.

If you'd like to find out more about this particular topic you can get a free copy of Expert Secrets that talks about this in more detail and gives some great examples.

Here's a link for you to get your free copy: bit.ly/cbg-freebook

Check your enquiry and payment processes

It's so important to make sure all your forms of enquiry are working correctly. Are telephone enquiries getting to you? Are web forms working? Are emails being responded to? Are all orders being received? Are payment pages working correctly? Web links can break, and message pads can be lost. Test them regularly to make sure the process is running smoothly.

Give them the 'WWWWWHC'

When advertising your product or service in any format, it is important to remember to include all the following:

1. Who is it ideal for?

2. Why is it beneficial for them?

3. What is involved?

4. Where is it located?

5. When does it takes place, or is it available?

6. How can they take part?

7. Call to action.

Google Maps

Make sure your business is officially listed on Google My Business by going to www.google.com/business. Once you've secured your business, make sure that all the relevant data is up-to-date, and you keep adding photos and encourage customers to review your business.

If you're looking for help to learn how to learn the basics of marketing your business, then I'd like to invite you to take part in our One Customer Away Coaching program. You can find out more by visiting: bit.ly/onecustomerawaycoaching

Assess your follow up process

It's so important to always check your follow up process. If you're using an automation service, are the tasks scheduling correctly and are you and your team completing those tasks in a timely manner? Are you continuing to follow up weeks later if the prospect still hasn't made a decision? Just because they haven't replied does not mean they are not interested. It's important to keep providing value and testimonials to those prospects until they either decide to buy or tell you they're not interested anymore.

Calls to action

Every piece of marketing you put out, including social media posts, should have some form of call to action (i.e. what to do next) - download the guide, like the page, get a free sample. Take a look through all of your marketing material and make sure you have a clear call to action.

First impressions count

Research shows that we only have less than seven seconds to make a good first impression. So a nice big smile with a firm handshake and a professional appearance are key. Remember, first impressions apply to any type of contact they have with your business. That might be your website, Facebook page, telephone call, or a member of your team. Take the time to review each one of these and ask the question - Is that a good first impression of my business?

Have a professional looking website

Having a professional looking website is key for me. It doesn't need to be flash, but it needs to have all the following included:

1. A clear description of you and your services

2. A nice and simple web address

3. Clear links to other pages

4. All your contact details (including social media links)

5. Photos of you and your setting

6. Testimonials

7. Clear call to action

8. Work on desktop and mobile

9. Up-to-date fresh quality content

10. Have the basic SEO information

In our business we still have a main website, but any time we do any type of advertising we don't take people to our traditional website. We now take them to a 'funnel'.

The problem with most traditional websites is that they leave the customer wondering around with no clear goal of what you want them to do (i.e. request information, check availability, etc.).

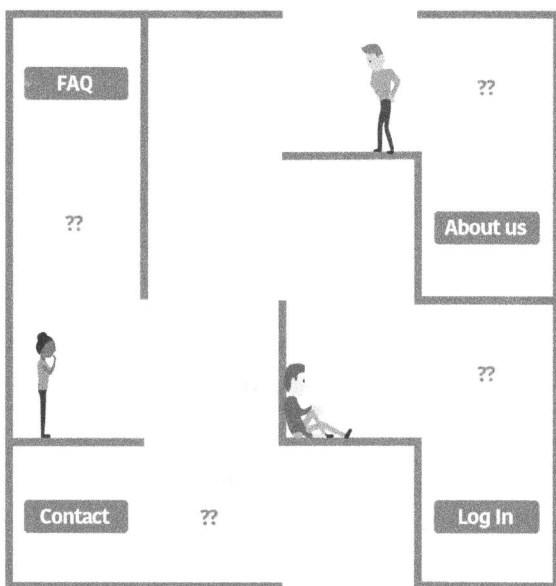

The whole idea of a funnel is to get as many of our target audience as possible to see our message and take some type of action.

You can pretty much use a sales funnel for every product or service. If you use the link below, you'll be able to find the perfect funnel for your business. Why not try it out to see just how easy it is to use, even if you've never touched a website before? It's that easy my eight-year-old son can use it.

If you'd like to find out more about funnels, then you can get a 14-day free trial to ClickFunnels by clicking the link below.

bit.ly/cmi-14day-trial

Speed of response

My personal opinion on this is the quicker you can get on to an enquiry, the better. If someone asks for an enquiry pack to be sent out, we try our very best to drop it at their home the very same day. Why? Because no one else is going to take the time to do that. It's easy; we have the packs prepared and drop them off on our way home from the business.

Map it Out

It's important to map out exactly where your customers come from. That way you'll know whether you are focusing your marketing efforts in the right area. The best way to do this is to purchase a custom map online and put your location right in the centre of it. Then map out where your existing customers come from. You might find that there are particular areas where the majority of your existing customers come from, so it would be worthwhile making a more targeted effort in those areas to share your message that lots of your existing customers already come from the area.

Other things to map out would be new housing developments, commercial areas, and where your competition are located. Use different colours for each reference. Doing this will not only give you a much better understanding of your geographical spread, but will highlight potential areas that you aren't really targeting.

PMMFS

We all want to be made to feel special and appreciated every now and again, so imagine if everyone was walking around with a Post-it Note on their head saying PMMFS - Please make me feel special.

Even if we're having a terrible day, we should always look for something positive to say when greeting another person. It helps build rapport and likeability and that one nice comment might get you another customer in the future.

Tracking your competition

It's so important to keep an eye on what your competition are doing. I'm not saying that you should copy them in any way, but they may be offering something that you hadn't thought of, or they may have a USP (unique selling proposition). What information are they sharing on social media? Have they changed their prices? If you know what your competition are doing, you can be better prepared when a prospect asks you how you compare to the competition. You'll also find that there are some businesses near you that are doing better than others, so it's important to know why. A great place to start is by liking their Facebook page and signing up to any newsletters or downloads that they have. Of course, you also want to ring them and get an idea of their pricing. If your competition is a very large business, then you may be able to find some of their example adverts on a tool called Similar Web, or Spyfu. These two tools allow you to type in the web addresses of your larger competitors and it gives you examples of what the competition is doing. It shows you examples of which adverts are doing well and where they are getting their website traffic from.

Make Time to Market

Marketing is often something that doesn't receive enough attention as most business owners are so busy trying to do everything. Your business may already be doing great, but that doesn't mean you should stop marketing your business as you need to keep your pipeline full of prospects for the future. It's far easier to maintain your marketing than letting it slack off and having to start all over again. Make sure you allocate time during your week appropriately. So, if your business is doing really well you won't need to allocate as much time as someone who is only struggling to get more customers.

Understand your market

Your business might be in a very deprived area, or you could be located in a very affluent area. You might be surrounded by large businesses or be in a heavily populated residential area. It's so important to understand the demographics of your area so you can adjust your strategy and marketing accordingly. My message to a heavily populated residential area would be completely different to if my business was surrounded by large businesses. My message would be more traditional for the residential areas, whereas for the businesses I'd be focussing on arranging corporate memberships or group discounts.

FAQs

Most prospective customers tend to ask the same questions, so when someone asks a new question, take the time to write down your best possible answer. Then take the time to learn those answers. That way you and your team will always be confident that you're all delivering the same high-quality answer.

Quick rebrand

A mini makeover could make the world of difference. A more modern font, bright colours and a strong current message that appeals to your exact audience can make a significant difference.

Feedback from lost customers

Ok, so your business isn't going to appeal to everyone, but it's so important to get feedback from people who didn't buy your product or service. It could be the price, the location, anything. You won't know unless you ask. Take the time to find this information out as it could be something putting potential customers off buying that you didn't even realise.

Create a marketing plan & calendar

We all get caught up in the day to day running of our business and can sometimes forget about marketing our businesses until it's almost too late. Planning ahead is crucial. It allows you to plan for peak enquiry times and make sure your campaigns are in place. You can plan your marketing accordingly based on events happening throughout the year, like holiday periods, or seasonal change. It's a great way to test different promotions throughout the year. You then want to breakdown your calendar into *Prospects* and *Existing Customers*. You may run a promotional offer for new prospects while you're running a referral program for your existing customers. Then you can look at splitting your marketing activity down into two further categories - *Evergreen* and *Monthly* promotions. Evergreen is activity that you consistently do on a monthly basis; whereas monthly campaigns tie into the holidays during that period.

Tracking your ROI

Tracking your Return on Investment (ROI) means are you tracking where your customer enquiries are coming from and which marketing campaigns got them to enquire. For example, you might get an enquiry from a search on Google, or another enquiry from another local business. If you're not asking the enquiry how they heard about you, then you've no idea which of your marketing efforts are working, so you could be wasting money. Every time a new enquiry comes in you should be tracking it.

Once you know where your enquiries are coming from you can then work out what it cost to get that enquiry. For example, if you spent £/$100 on Facebook ads in the month and you got ten new enquiries from Facebook, and one of them bought your product or service. Let's say the value of that customer was worth £/$5,000 for the year, that would mean you generated £/$5,000 from £/$100 in ad spend, giving you a 500% return on investment. Now if that customer stays with you for another three years, that would mean you've got a 1,500% return on investment! That's huge, all from a £/$100 ad spend on Facebook. Now you know you've got a great return from that marketing source and you can now see that it's easily worth putting more money into Facebook ads. Tracking is vital to know where to spend your money.

Tracking Phone Numbers

Tracking numbers allow you to set up a designated phone line for each piece of marketing you have. That way you can track exactly the number of phone calls you have received, and which marketing is working best for you. You can also keep track of how many calls you missed and what times those calls were coming in. That way you can hold your team accountable. The majority of companies offering this service provide you with the opportunity to listen to all the calls, so you can find out exactly what questions prospects are asking and then create the best possible response to those questions. It's not only a great way to track what marketing works, it's a great way to help train your team and improve your telephone skills.

Build Your List

I always use this scenario to help people get an understanding of how important lists are and where they should be stored. Just imagine all your files went up on fire and you had no records of enquiries or your existing customers. Storing lists online in a CRM (Customer Relationship Management) system is crucial. That way if anything was to ever go wrong with paper-based copies, or files on your computer, you have everything stored online. The next thing is to segment your list into various groups. For example, current existing customers, past customers, current enquiries, past enquiries that didn't purchase, people interested in a more expensive product or service, people who have downloaded free guides or reports, etc. The more you segment your list, the more you can tailor your message to speak to that exact person. You may want to send out a referral campaign to existing and past customers, but the message you would use to engage them would need to be different.

We use a great CRM system for all of our lists that's easy to use and priced accordingly to your budget.

You can find out more and get a 14-day free trial by visiting:

bit.ly/cmi-active-campaign

Be found on the Map

It's so important to make sure you are listed on the main search engines like Google, Bing and Yahoo, so start by searching your business name and location on all the major search engines. You should be found by your business name, but then search 'what you provide in your location' and see whether you still come up. One way to make sure you start appearing is using keywords and tags on your website and any blog articles that you have. Be sure to use keywords that your potential customer would use to find your product or service. Ask a friend what words they would use.

Want to learn the basics of how to market your business?

If you're looking for help to learn how to learn the basics of marketing your business, then I'd like to invite you to take part in our One Customer Away Coaching program. You can find out more by visiting: bit.ly/onecustomerawaycoaching

Develop Your Relationships

Introduction

So, you've got a new customer but now maintaining great communication with the customer is going to be essential to not only ensure they stay happy and informed, but to whether they recommend you to friends and family. There's no point spending money on marketing if you're going to be losing them once they've become a customer. In this section, we're going to take a look at ways you can develop your relationships with your customers and then encourage them to recommend you to others.

Cash referrals

One of the most powerful strategies we've ever used is cash referrals. So if someone refers a new customer, they get a cash referral relevant to the value of that customer's transaction. It could be a simple structure like a percentage of the first sale, or a monthly recurring amount.

Here's an example. A Day Care parent recommends another parent to join. So, if someone refers a new starter, they get £/$30 for the number of days they are attending each week. So, if a new child joins for three days per week off the back of a referral, the referring parent gets £/$90 cash. Would you be happy acquiring a new customer for only £/$90? Of course, it has to be relevant to the amount the customer will spend with you; but that's nothing in comparison to how much money that parent is going to spend with that business during their time as a customer. Take this to the next level by making sure you take a picture of you giving the money to the customer and then share it on Facebook and tag them. You'll get more of your existing customers referring, and you'll also find the person receiving the cash will usually bring you in additional referrals very quickly over the next few weeks because you've motivated them to do so.

Collect referral stamps

You've probably seen those cards given by coffee shops - get a stamp every time you buy a coffee, then when you collect 10, you get a free coffee. Well, the same principle applies to customers making referrals.

Create your own referral card, when they make ten referrals they get 1 of 5 choices as an ultimate reward (everyone has different tastes, so they won't be all motivated by the same incentive). So still give them cash for each referral, but when they get to 10 referrals, reward them with something special.

Give your team the best incentives

Whatever referral incentives you have in place for your customers, take that to a higher level for your team. I would recommend increasing it by at least 20-30%. It's a great way to show your team that you really care about them and a great opportunity to earn additional cash and get them to really praise your business to their friends and family.

Golden tickets

Remember the golden tickets from the film *Charlie and the Chocolate Factory*? Everyone was after those golden tickets, so you could create your own version of this. Every time a new customer enrols in your business you give them two golden tickets that they can share with any of their friends or family looking for your product or service.

The golden ticket entitles the new customer to some type of special offer, while the referring customer gets an equally great offer. It always generates a huge amount of interest from their family and friends and could lead to a new regular customer. You could make it into a PR story. Of course, there needs to be terms and conditions around this, but it's up to you to determine what they are.

Badges

I got this idea originally from a well-known theme park in Florida. They have people working there from all around the world, so not only do they have the person's name on the badge, they also have where they're from. It has a huge impact, as people see the badges and strike up a conversation either because they're from the same place, they know someone there, or they're genuinely interested. We didn't think it would have the same impact on our business when we first started using them, as all the team are from within a 15-mile radius, but we were surprised to see the number of conversations it triggered amongst customers and the team. So, include your logo, name, location, and perhaps something quirky about that person. I guarantee it will get people talking inside and outside of your business.

Share your stories

The first piece of marketing I ever created for our business was our origin story because people buy from people and not companies, and they become more engaged and trusting when they can relate to you. I wanted customers to know exactly why we set up our business. I wanted them to know that my wife was so nervous about going back to work and leaving our children in the care of a stranger, and we couldn't find a childcare provider locally that had the same ethos as us. I wanted them to know our mission and our bigger purpose. I wanted them to feel more connected to us as the owners and feel they have that personal relationship. Now there are lots of stories that you can tell, such as: Why you decided to open your own business, why you fell in love with your industry, why you've picked the great team that work with you based on their stories. These stories help to develop a relationship with the prospect, so take the time to write out your stories and share them with everyone.

If you struggle with writing any type of content, here is a link to a great tool we use. You plug in your keywords into the boxes and it creates your stories and sales copy for you. Click the link to find out more:

bit.ly/funnelscripts-freetrial

Incentivise reviews

Reviews (social proof) from others is far more effective than us saying something good about our own business. One of the ways to get more reviews is to incentivise your customers. We produced a postcard that we hand out to five customers each week. Putting reviews on gradually throughout the year is far better for Google and Facebook rather than asking everyone in the business to do them all at once. It's a lot easier to chase customers when you are only chasing a few each week. The postcard asks the customers to leave reviews on our top four websites, including Google and Facebook. If the customer completes all four reviews, they get a $15 gift card as a thank you. If the customer makes a particular reference to a member of the team, the team member gets an extra $15.

It's easy for a customer to complete and they are incentivised to do it. If we receive ten reviews in a month, our team get an extra bonus. Making the process as simple as possible for the customer is key, so rather than make the customer search for our business on each of the platforms, we created a short bitly link directly to the specific page. That way, all they had to do was copy the short URL link and it would take them straight to the appropriate page. We also schedule an email to go out directly to the customer with all four links included so all they need to do it click the link.

Would you like help with your marketing?

If you'd like to find out how to implement these ideas into your business head on over to www.creations.marketing to check out our range of coaching programs and 'done for you' services.

Phone Enquiry

Introduction

The phone enquiry is often a part that lets a lot of businesses down and can often be someone's first contact with your business, so it's key to making a great first impression. In this section, we're going to take a look at how to deal with a phone enquiry, how to get all the information we need from the caller, and how to give the caller the best possible experience during the call.

Answer the phone

Missing a phone call can mean missing out on a customer that could be worth a huge amount to your business, so it's crucial to make sure your phone always gets answered. Of course, there might be the odd exception where you can't get to the phone, so if you know there may be times when you can't answer the phone, then you need to put backup processes in place.

Some businesses divert their phones to a professional call handling service if they don't manage to answer in 5 rings. The answering service uses the same script as the business and then pass the message on to the management team via a text and email. Another option is to have an auto attendant when someone rings - so instead of the traditional dial tone, your customer immediately gets greeted by a professional voiceover asking the caller to bear with you as someone is currently on the phone, then include some promotional messages about your business while the caller is waiting. This is all going on while the phone is still ringing in your business and waiting for someone to pick up. That way it buys you a bit more time if you are busy. Of course, you'll still need to have a professional voicemail for out of hours and those odd occasions when you just can't get to the phone.

Phone script

The goal for all new telephone enquiries is to get the enquirer's contact details and then to get them ideally come in to your business. The problem is that when you're working in your business, you're never just on the phone. Your team might all be dealing with customers. You and your team need to have a structure to follow, so no matter what's going on, you know the information you've got to get. There are six core steps that will ensure you get what you need and the caller leaves with a great impression of your business and professionalism.

1. Give them an AMAZING introduction - You want your prospect to hear the excitement in your voice that you're so pleased that they've called, and you'd like to be the first to welcome them to your business.

2. Discovery - Where you find out why they called you and where they got your information from.

3. Rapport building - Where you take the time to listen to the prospect and show compassion.

4. Communicate your unique mechanism - What's unique about your business compared to the competition?

5. Book the appointment - It's important that you book the appointment or get their contact information to send out your prospect pack.

6. The close - Making sure you've answered any of their questions and they're happy and looking forward to meeting you.

Train your team on how to handle a phone enquiry

It's so important to train your team on how to handle an enquiry over the phone, or in person. I've been in some businesses where team members won't answer the phone when the manager is away as they are too scared to do so. It just comes down to providing the appropriate training to your team. Use part of your team meetings to always rehearse the script and role play. You could provide your staff with a certification for completing sales training (in telephone enquiries and face to face), which could be used towards their CPD.

Enquiry tracking sheets

This sheet is one of the most important documents to me. The whole idea of the tracking sheet is to ensure we capture all the relevant information from the prospect during the call and to find out exactly how they heard about us. Knowing this is crucial to determine which of our marketing efforts are working the best, so we can invest more into them. These enquiry tracking sheets should be located around your business, so they're easy to grab when an enquiry comes in.

Incentivise them to book an appointment / tour

Remember our goal from the phone enquiry is to get the prospect's contact details and get them to take action. This might be to get them to make an appointment to come in and meet us. Some enquiries maybe a little hesitant at first, so it's important to have a few incentives that you can offer to encourage them to say yes. You could start by telling them you only have three slots left for appointments this next week as you're getting a lot of new enquiries, or inform the prospect that your availability is very limited, so you'd really encourage them securing an appointment before they're all taken (we always want something more if there's a chance we're going to miss out on it). Then you could offer them a free gift if they arrange an appointment there and then on the phone.

On hold audio

If you ever have to put a customer or prospect on hold at any time, make sure you've got a professional audio recording that they can listen to that plays calming music and talks about any offers or promotions you've got going on in your setting. You can get these call recordings produced very easily through 'on hold' audio companies. There's a great company I'd recommend using that has done all of our automated answering and the owner has created a special offer for all readers. Head on over to: bit.ly/inarrator

Do you want to learn basic marketing for your business?

If you're looking for help to learn how to learn the basics of marketing your business, then I'd like to invite you to take part in our One Customer Away Coaching program. You can find out more by visiting: bit.ly/onecustomerawaycoaching

The Appointment

Introduction

This is the part that can either secure you the prospect, or if it doesn't go well, the prospect could end up telling others about their bad experience, so it's crucial to get this right. We're going to look at the whole experience. I'd encourage you to check yourself off against each one of these and give yourself a rating of 0 - 5. (0 = not doing it at all, right the way up to 5 = fully in place and happy). That way you can always come back and check your progress against each point. Let's get started.

Pre-appointment call

It's always a good idea to call the prospect a few hours before the planned appointment just to make sure they are still coming and confirm they know where they are going.

Please their senses

Think about the last time you walked into a new restaurant and how you created your first impressions of that business. First, you may have judged them on how it looked from the outside. Did it look clean and welcoming? Then as you walked in you would have been hit by the smell. Did the smell of delicious food excite you, or was there a smell of burnt food in the air? What did it sound like? Was it loud with great music or was it so quiet you could hear a pin drop? Did you have to stand up to wait for a table or did you have a comfy sofa to enjoy some pre-dinner drinks? Finally, the food, how did it taste? Was it warm? Did it fill you up? I'm sure you can relate to those sensations, and the same applies to when someone is viewing your setting. So, use the following to see how you do against the five senses:

SIGHT - What do people see as they approach your business and when they enter the building? Is it bright and colourful, clean and tidy, and somewhere you'd like to enter?

SMELL - As you open the door, what does it smell like? Is it fresh and inviting or musky?

SOUND - Have you got calming music playing? Or are you drowned out by other sounds?

TASTE - Do you provide your prospects with a drink and perhaps some biscuits when they arrive?

TOUCH - Have you got somewhere comfortable for the prospect to sit when they come in or are they stuck standing in the hall?

All these senses have a considerable impact on your prospect's first impressions of you and your business, so it's important to regularly assess yourself against these and always be looking for ways you can improve on them.

Thank-you cards work wonders

If you've got any thank you cards from happy customers make sure you have them clearly displayed for your new prospects to see when they arrive at your business. It's more social proof that you provide a great service.

Personalised greeting note in reception

I picked this idea up from visiting my old accountant. Every time I would go there they would have a personalised message for me upon arrival. So, if you know you've got an appointment today make a personalised welcome message for the prospect - 'Welcome Maria to _____'. During the rest of the time, you could just have a generic welcome message to welcome everyone into the building. A great way of doing this is on a light box or a black board.

Use their name

If you know you have an appointment booked, make sure your team knows the name of the prospect. Addressing someone by their name gives them comfort and makes you look more competent. According to research, hearing our name lights up different parts of our brain that no other words do. It helps you like the person addressing you by your name and makes you feel more important. So, make sure you and your team know the name of the prospect before they attend their appointment.

Video card in reception

When a prospect first arrives at your business, a great way to ensure they know what you're all about it to sit them down with a drink and let them watch a video card while they get settled in. A video card is like an A4 brochure with a video inside. You can include a video from you introducing the business and what you're all about, testimonials from customers, and perhaps some short videos from key members of your team. The videos can easily be changed if you have a new message you want to get across. It's a great way to introduce your business and leave the prospect watching for a few moments while you do final preparations for your appointment.

Find out exactly what they're looking for in a product or service

Traditionally when a prospect attends an appointment we are eager to share everything about why our business is so wonderful, but we are missing the most important step. We need to find out exactly what the prospect is looking for. They may have had a terrible experience with another business, or this may be the very first business they've viewed. So, before starting your appointment, sit down with the prospect and ask them open-ended questions about what they are looking for. You'll be surprised at how much they open up. Now that you know exactly what they're looking for and what their concerns are, you can make sure you address those points in the appointment.

Get everyone to shake hands

In a world where customer service is declining more than ever, I would make it compulsory that everyone you introduce to the prospect on the tour shakes the prospect's hand. It portrays confidence in you and your team and it's another thing that will help separate you from the competition.

Give a goodie bag

We all love receiving gifts, so at the end of the appointment give the prospect a goodie bag with some branded merchandise and perhaps some samples depending on your product or service. If you work with local business partners, you could include some inexpensive items or samples from them. It's another way to set you apart from the competition and get them talking about you.

Mail a gift

If you don't manage to get the prospect to sign up or buy there and then, you could mail out a gift the very next day. This could be something simple like chocolates and a letter to the prospect saying it was great to meet them and reconfirming anything they raised during the appointment. It helps show that you really would love to have them as a customer and you don't just see them as another enquiry.

Your appearance

This might sound obvious, but do you have a strict policy on uniform and staff appearance? It all reflects on how the customer judges you on their first impression. If your team's uniform is looking old and dirty, prospects may start to question what other things are slipping within your business. What happens when your staff leave for the day? Do they continue to wear their uniform? Because their actions outside of work will reflect on you if they are still wearing it. Having a strict policy in place on the standards you expect can really help to make a great first impression on anyone that comes in contact with your brand.

Ask for the sale

This often scares a lot of people when it comes to asking for money, but you have to look at it from a different angle. If you think your product or service is right for the customer, then you have a duty of care to ask for the sale. It's important to finish the appointment by bringing them to a quiet room/area where you can ask for the sale. Tell the prospect why you think your product or service is perfect for them, based on what they told you they were looking for at the start. This will be uncomfortable at first but the more you practice this, the more you'll get used to it. Remember if you think you've got the best solution for that customer, you have a duty to ask for the sale.

The follow up

You may show prospects around your business who just simply aren't ready to buy yet. They may have only just started their search. So, having a thorough follow up campaign is crucial to keep in touch and secure that sale when they are ready to buy. Ideally, this needs to be an automated system that schedules reminders and sends emails for you and arranges a series of follow up tasks.

Active Campaign is a great system to do this. You can find out more and get a 14-day free trial by visiting:

http://bit.ly/cmi-active-campaign

Social Media

Introduction

There are over three billion internet users, and over two billion of those have active social media accounts. The way we communicate with our audience has changed forever and avoiding social media as a business is no longer an option. The great news is social media provides your business with so many advantages over those businesses who are not embracing it to its full potential. In this section, we're going to take a look at why social media is so important and how you can use it to market your business.

Facebook business page

Setup a Facebook business page first, that way you can keep your personal and professional profiles separate. Here are some of the great reasons to have a business page.

1. You get increased exposure to potential customers.

2. You can gather more leads through your page by linking to enquiry forms.

3. You don't pay anything to have it.

4. You can start to run Facebook ads and reach your specific target audience.

5. You can drive more traffic to your website.

6. You can share events you've got coming up and invite people to attend.

7. You can keep an eye on your competition and how their page is growing.

8. You can use Facebook insights to get a better understanding of your page.

Facebook posts

It's important to keep your content relevant to your target audience. Remember, you may have different types of customers with different interests, so it's important to share content that's relevant to everyone. So, start with all the basics like:

1. Promote events and post photos from those events.

2. Host competitions and announce the winners.

3. Share tips and ideas on ways to use your products and services.

4. Share photos of things you are proud of within your business.

5. Showing photos from charity fundraising also helps to raise awareness for the charity you are supporting.

6. Post around four times per week and keep the content fresh. Opinions are different on this, but we've typically found around lunchtime and 7-8pm gets the best engagement.

Facebook insights

This is a powerful tool provided by Facebook that gives you easy to understand data about users on your Facebook fan page or group. You can track post engagements, which is a great way to see what your audience is reacting to. You can also look at the demographics of the users liking your page (gender, country, age range). Knowing this data allows you to tailor your message and then target your ads to appeal to more of the same audience.

Google analytics

This allows you to look at data on the users of your website. You need to copy the Google code onto your website first, but then you'll be able to look at all the demographic data of users and the flow of how someone has gone through your website. You can see which pages are more popular and where people drop off, and you have the option to retarget them based on actions they did or did not take.

Optimise your bio

Adding keywords to your bio will help you show up more often in search results. Include phrases that your audience will be searching for.

Encourage check-ins

You could design a simple backdrop that encourages people to take selfies or share photos on Instagram and Facebook. You could run competitions rewarding customers for the most shares, or the best selfie pic using your custom backdrop.

Run competitions

There are plenty of people you could ask for freebies from including suppliers or local businesses, particularly those looking to promote their services to your audience. Plan out a competition at least once a month and relate it to a theme going on at that time.

Promote your audience, not you

We all love a bit of praise from others, particularly when our friends and family get to see it. So, help them out! Congratulate customers for taking part and attending events, entering competitions; anything where you can praise them and tag them so friends and family get to see. If you have team members, praise and reward them as well. Your audience is far more likely to share these posts over self-promotion, and it shows you care about your customers and your team.

There's always room for self-promotion

I know this slightly contradicts my previous point, but I have a reason. If you've got good news stories, or you're offering a new add-on service, go ahead and promote it. After all, you're a business, but it ideally needs to be something newsworthy that your customer will find interesting.

Tap in to communities / tribes

Where do your 'ideal customers' hang out? Marketing isn't just about promotion and "Me Me Me". It's important to interact and add value. Start hanging around where your ideal customers are - face to face locations or online in Facebook groups, or in Twitter chats, just to name a few. Once you join those communities, start helping others and adding value wherever possible. The more you help others, the more people will start to know, like, and trust you and promote you to others. You'll also start to see what problems or desires those customers have, which can then allow you to tailor your products and services accordingly.

Boost your Facebook posts

If you see people are liking and engaging with your posts on Facebook, start to boost them as a paid advert. It's a really easy process to follow and you choose who you want that boost to be shown to. So, people similar to your existing customers, people who have liked your page, people within a certain area and age range, etc.

Ask people to share

There are lots of ways we can encourage people to share things, but one of the most successful ways is by playing on people's emotions. So, if you've got good news stories, or perhaps you're looking to raise money for a local charity, then people are more likely to share this over a post that is trying to sell a service.

Engage in conversations

If you've tagged a customer on a post to congratulate or praise them for something, you'll often find that friends and family will like and comment on that post. You can then message that person and encourage them to like your Facebook page.

Ask for referrals

This is one of those things that we often forget to do or avoid doing for fear of making the customer feel awkward. A simple way to do this is add a Call to Action (CTO) at the bottom of the post asking them to share it with others who they think might be interested.

Run a poll

One of the best ways to get feedback and engagement from your group is to run a quick poll. You may want to get an idea for your next blog, so ask them what topics they would like covered and give them some suggestions. It's important to respond promptly though and praise people for joining in and contributing.

Post content frequently and encourage engagement

Some people think that they don't have enough to share with others, or they don't feel they've got anything to share at all. One of the things we need to realise is that we've got a lot of knowledge in our heads on our particular product or service that potential customers don't know. Just because we know it, doesn't mean our potential customers know it, so they'll appreciate you sharing helpful information.

Schedule posts

The last thing you want to be doing is manually sending all of your social media posts out, especially when there are some great online systems that will do this all for you, like Hootsuite and Sprout Social. These platforms are easy to set up, you just copy and paste your content, along with the photo, and you tell it when to send the post. Right now, the best time to post is usually lunchtime and in the evenings when people are not in work, so make the most of scheduling your posts, so you also get a bit of downtime.

Use Facebook Live or Instagram Stories

Facebook loves video, so if you can share content live with your audience, there's more chance of people seeing it over a static post. You can also boost it later if the video gets a good response. Another option could be to record a live tour of your business. Share stories adding value and sharing your knowledge with your audience.

Survey customers

Getting customer feedback is crucial. The great thing with online surveys is customers are more likely to respond when they've got time and they're scrolling through Facebook, rather than asking them for feedback as they're rushing out the door. We regularly get lots of comments from the customers around how they love being involved in the decision process, so it's a great communication and feedback tool.

Facebook team page

If you've got members of staff, set up a team Facebook group for them. It's a great way to bring the team together to share ideas and praise them at random times to show them how much you value them. You can run team competitions on there. If you're looking to add a new product or service, we'll often run polls on there asking their opinion. That way they know they've got a say in the decision-making process and they generally tend to be more open on the page instead of asking them face to face. It's easy to set up and can really help motivate your team.

Facebook Pixel

The Facebook Pixel is a piece of HTML code (website coding) that you copy and paste onto your website. It allows you and Facebook to track what people are doing on your website and the type of people visiting your website. That way, if you ever decide to run Facebook ads to your website, Facebook will already have a good understanding of the type of people that are likely to take action on your website, and they'll show your ads to more people in that target audience.

A good way to check if you've got the pixel code installed on your website is by downloading the Facebook Pixel Helper. This is a little icon that sits on your internet browser and shows you if the code is installed on your pages.

Facebook bot messenger

Facebook Messenger bot gives you a private message channel directly to your user. The message appears straight away in their Messenger app, so it's a great way to get past all the clutter of email and social media. You'll need an existing Facebook page to set up its bot functionality and you'll need administrator rights on the page. You can answer customer enquiries in seconds and send out offers, promotions, and events to your existing list. There are lots of companies offering this tool and one we are using at the time of writing this book is www.manychat.com

LinkedIn

Even though LinkedIn is mainly for business to business use, it's important not to dismiss it as a great marketing tool. You never know who might decide to take a look at your profile, so it's important to keep it up to date with all your professional qualifications and any testimonials you can get from other business professionals that you have worked with. You'll then want to set up a business page that shares all your core content - company introduction, what you're about, and any contact details. Share your blog articles on your page. It all helps position you as the local expert. If you decide to target corporate companies in the future, you've now got a good presence online that they can review and they may be more likely to take you seriously when you approach them.

YouTube channel

At the time of writing this book, almost five billion videos are watched on YouTube every single day and over 300 hours of video are uploaded to YouTube every minute. So, if you're not on YouTube, you're missing out on a big opportunity. YouTube is owned by Google, so having videos on YouTube that are set up with the relevant keywords will help your listing. Set up your own YouTube channel and get uploading. There's lots of great content you could share on there.

Would you like help with your marketing?

If you'd like to find out how to implement these ideas into your business head on over to www.creations.marketing to check out our range of coaching programs and 'done for you' services.

Direct Mail & Gift Ideas

Introduction

Over the last few years, the amount of direct mail we receive from companies has been decreasing, but in recent times it seems to have flipped full-circle. Businesses have realised that since the general public is receiving less, they're more likely to open it when it does arrive and looks enticing. Did you know that Google advertises their Google Pay Per Click service to business via direct mail? So, if the online giant of advertising is using direct mail, there's clearly something in it. In this section, we're going to take a look at the various ways you can communicate with your enquiries and existing customers via direct mail, so let's get stuck in.

Lumpy mail

Most of us like getting mail, as long as it's not a bill, but we're even more intrigued when it's something bulky. We just have to open it out of curiosity. There are lots of great little products you can put in the mail. The key is to tie your marketing message back to the product.

For example, you could send them a sand time with a core message around "time is running out to secure your discounted offer". You're pretty much guaranteed someone is going to open it, so you need to make sure you've got that strong message inside and remember to follow up a day after it arrives.

Mailing out products

I talk about this in the Lead Magnet section in more detail, but if you've run an advert giving away sample products, that person has given you their address details and is expecting the product to be shipped to them. So, when you mail the product out to them, you could include a quick introduction to your setting and make sure your message relates to the product.

Flyers to popular areas

If you've identified through your map areas where a high number of existing customers come from, be sure to mail them regularly with different promotions letting them know others in the area are already using your services. Be sure to always include a call to action - 'Go to _____ to download your voucher worth _____. Hurry though as there's only 20 available'.

Greeting cards

How many businesses that you buy a product or service from actually do anything for your birthday, or Mother's Day? Ok, they may send you an automated email, but that's about it. What if you sent out a handwritten card for each celebration? How special would that make your customers feel? They're more than likely to tell a lot of their friends and share it on social media. It's a small gesture but will really make your customers feel happy.

Stationery

Let's face it, most of us love receiving new stationery and resources, so it's great if you can apply your logo and then give out your branded stationary to your existing customers, prospects, and local businesses on your dream 100 list. That way you're giving them all something for free, but in return they are spreading knowledge of your business to their network.

Bags

Giving a branded bag out when a new customer starts working with your business is a great little thank you gift that customers will love to have. You then get several customers being seen with your branded bags around your local area.

Free t-shirts

More and more businesses are giving away free t-shirts to customers to help them feel part of the business, particularly when the business has a great culture that the customers can get behind.

Postcards

We talked about postcards earlier, but another way to use a postcard is if you're running an event that you want your existing customers to help you promote. Have the postcards pre-written and stamped, then give them to your existing customers to send out to their friends and family to invite them to the event on your behalf. The new enquiry then brings that postcard with them, and the existing customer gets a special thank you gift in return.

Want more help with your marketing?

If you'd like to find out how to implement these ideas into your business head on over to www.creations.marketing to check out our range of coaching programs.

Paid Advertising

Introduction

In the past everyone needed big advertising budgets to get their message out to their audience, but that's all changed. Digital opportunities are available to every business, they're easier to track and can deliver a great return on investment (ROI) and they allow you to increase or decrease the amount you spend at the click of a button. So, if your business is full you could decide to decrease your ad spend, or you could increase it if your customer numbers are low. Here are some ideas on how to use paid advertising in your business.

Facebook advertisements

Facebook ads are adverts you create to target your ideal customer online and are displayed on either the news feed or on the right-hand column on a desktop, or on the news feed on mobile. Here are some of the reasons why Facebook advertising can be such a great investment:

- Audience targeting - You can create custom audiences based on things people have declared.

- Easy to setup - The structure to set up ads and campaigns is not much different than making a regular Facebook post, so you don't need advance knowledge or code to get it started.

- Low cost - Even though the cost is rising as more businesses turn to Facebook ads, the cost is still relatively cheap to reach your target audience with this level of accuracy.

- Retargeting - You have the ability to retarget people based on what actions they have taken and choose what content to show them.

- Socially engaging - If someone else has already liked the ad, it provides social proof to others.

- Variety of ad options - You can use still images or videos to test which work better for your target audience.

- You can upload existing customer data and ask Facebook to find similar potential customers through their search function.

Facebook has a huge amount of additional demographic information that other platforms simply don't have. For example, they know gender, geographic location, age, relationship status, education, and profession. This is just to name a few, but I've included a list below of some of the information you can use to target your audience on Facebook. Here are some of the targeting options Facebook has to offer:

- Location

- Age - the ability to select an age range DEMOGRAPHICS –

- Gender - male, female or all

- Languages - any language

- Relationship - 'Interested in' or 'Relationship Status'
- Education - level, field of study and schools and undergrad years
- Work - employers, job title, industries,
- Home - home type, home ownership, household composition
- Generation - Baby boomers, Generation X, Millennials

Interests • Business & Industry - banking, construction, small businesses • Entertainment - Games, live events, movies • Family & Relationships - fatherhood, motherhood, marriage, parenting • Fitness & Wellness - dieting, gyms, nutrition • Food & drink - beverages, cooking, cuisine, restaurants • Hobbies & Activities - arts and music, home and garden, pets, travel, vehicles • Shopping & Fashion - beauty, clothing, shopping, toys • Sports & Outdoors - Outdoor recreation or sports • Technology - computers, or consumer electronics

Behaviours • Business To Business - Industry or company size • Charitable donations - type of charity • Expats - multiple countries • Financial - banking, investments • Mobile Device User - by brand and type of device • Purchase behaviour - types of things they buy • Travel - business or personal, family vacations, frequent flyers • This isn't everything, but it gives you an idea of how detailed you can get with your targeting.

Facebook retargeting

Once you've got the Facebook pixel installed on your website you can start to run Facebook retargeting ads to those that landed on certain pages of your website but didn't land on others. Think about it, how many times have you been looking at something on the internet, got distracted and then forgotten all about it? This allows you to show reminder ads to those that didn't get to the page you wanted. So, someone might start to download a free report from your website but didn't get to the thank you page. You could show them that report through an ad and link them back to that specific page. It's a very powerful tool when it's used correctly.

Google PPC

This is one of my favourite advertising platforms. Why? Even though the cost might be slightly higher than other platforms, it allows you to target people who are actually interested in your services and are actively looking right now. So, if someone is on Google and types in 'The best _____ in [your city] they are more than likely trying to find a business that provides the service in that area. They are actually looking for information right now. That's why Google PPC is great, because you are targeting someone who is actively looking for what you provide. Go to Google and type in your product or service in your town, and see what comes up. You may find some of your competitors are already advertising on there, so make a note of what they are saying in their adverts. You may find no one is using PPC, so it's a great opportunity for you to take the number one spot.

Make a list of words and phrases you think a customer would type in if they were looking for your product or service in your area. Type those words and phrases into Google and see what other ideas come up. If you can't find an advert - make your search a little bigger, so you include a local city. There's bound to be someone using PPC then. Have a look at what they've got written in their ads, so it gives you an idea of what to include in your advert. Remember to be specific on location when you're setting up your ads. The last thing you want to do is show your ads to someone living 100 miles away from you. I wouldn't spend too much right out of the gate. Start with £5-£10 per day if it's your first time using Google PPC. Keep a close eye on how they are performing. Google is great at giving you feedback.

It will show you which keywords you appeared for and what people clicked on and a whole heap of other information. You can also adjust your bidding and daily spend. Google PPC is definitely one of the best forms of advertising by far.

YouTube Advertising

YouTube has over 1.5 billion users and is the world's second most used search engine at the time of writing this book. It's the third most visited website after Google and Facebook. YouTube adverts are generally still cheap.

Targeting on YouTube is very good, you can target your audience by age, gender, keywords, and other things they may be interested in. However, that's just the beginning. You can show your ads on specific videos and channels. So, if you know your prospects are looking at videos specifically relating to your product or service, or a competitor, you can get your video ad in front of them.

Partnership and Networking

Introduction

One of the biggest realisations I ever had in marketing was that someone else has already got my ideal customers. Think about it, your potential customers are already using other products and services. You just need to find out what those products and services are. Partnering with others allows you to build your network and access their customers via a referral directly from the business they are already buying from. Let's take a look at a few examples.

Dream 100

Your ideal customer is already someone else's customer, so they're already buying products or services from someone else. I call these businesses part of my *Dream 100 list*. They are all businesses that already have my ideal customer and I want to create a relationship with that business, so if their customer is ever looking for my product or service, they'll recommend me. This can include any business that already has your ideal customer and doesn't offer the same product or service as you. Building a relationship with your Dream 100 list is key to get them referring into your business.

Interview them

If some of your dream 100 have large followings online, you could ask to interview them on a podcast or on a Facebook live. The great benefit here is that you get exposure to their audience, you build a relationship with your partner, and your customers get access to the free content you have recorded.

Attend local networking events

Chamber of Commerce and BNI are great examples of networking events. These are all great opportunities for you to make other local businesses aware of your business and demonstrate how and why you stand out from the competition. You'll be surprised how many of the other businesses attending already have your ideal customers and could refer you quite a lot of business. Who knows, you may find a business service there that you need.

Get interviewed

There are a number of ways to do this. First of all, you need to contact the radio stations and position yourself as the local expert and if they ever need someone to interview on your related topics, then you are happy to help. The same applies to television with more local television stations popping up, so it's easier than ever to get on television. You have to have the brass balls to contact these channels and offer your services as the local expert, but the publicity from it can have a major impact on your business. The second way to do this is if you've got a strong opinion on something that's topical right now, then make your opinions known. Don't sit on the fence. Share your opinion and let others know how you feel. It may get picked up by the media.

Contribute to publications

Editors are always under pressure to produce content. They'll happily publish quality articles for free. What publications and blogs do your ideal customers read? Find out, then reach out to get in front of them. Don't worry if you're not good at writing content. You don't have to write it yourself. You could hire someone to do this for you as a ghost writer. You tell them exactly what you want, and they write it for you. You then have content ready to share to other publications.

Affiliate programs

This is another form of joint venture; similar to the Dream 100 List, but usually all these partnerships will be after is a commission in return. These types of partners exist in two core areas: Those with a big following in your sector, simply looking to promote a product in return for a payment, and those that are affiliates for a living. They will actively go out and promote your brand on your behalf through various forms of advertising, again in return for a commission payment. The important thing to remember here though is you give them strict parameters on what they can and cannot say. The benefit is that you have a sales team at your disposal, but only pay them for sales.

Contact large local businesses

Getting your services listed on the employee benefits program is a great way of potentially accessing a lot of customers. The employer will be looking at why they should partner with you, so having an exclusive offer is going to be key to selling your product or service to the decision makers. Another important factor is making sure that your package is right for them. Think about how your product or service solves a problem for them. Once you've got a partnership in place, you really want to try to arrange a presentation to anyone interested. You could perhaps do this during their lunch hour, or they may invite you along to employer fairs. Make sure you take plenty of professional marketing and have your offer ready to present. This probably isn't going to be something that happens overnight, but you never know, you may call an employer at the right time when they're looking for a solution.

Write for the local media

This is a great way to be positioned as a local expert. Local media - newspapers, articles, websites and blogs - are always looking for content. Don't be afraid to be confident in your opinion. There's no money in being neutral, so if you have an opinion on something, be proud to share your thoughts, knowledge, and opinions. You'll get lovers and maybe some haters, but you'll start to position yourself as the local expert very quickly.

Partner referrals

One of my favourite films is *Miracle of 34th Street* and I'll always remember the part in the film where Coles would help their customers find a product elsewhere if they didn't stock it themselves. I'm not suggesting you tell customers to go to another business, but you may not cater for a particular customer, or that particular product they are looking for. If you're working in partnership with another similar business and recommend them potential customers, then they may feel obliged to do the same in return. If someone does something nice for you, you feel obliged to give back. Of course, you need to build this relationship, but I have seen this happening in a few businesses and both partners benefit from the relationship.

Community Marketing

Introduction

There are so many opportunities to develop relationships with your local community, and the great thing is, it's going to cost you hardly anything except time, but will bring you a great return on your investment. How great would it feel if someone new to your community asked about where to find the best supplier of your product or service and everyone highly recommended you? That's the benefit of community marketing, so let's take a look at how you can develop these relationships.

Monthly cake runs

Wouldn't it be nice if you were a local business that received a treat once a month from a local business like you? A great way to do this is to schedule a cake run. Select 5-10 businesses on your Dream 100 list and take them out a box of treats once a month. You could buy them from a local baker (one of your VIP partners). It's important to do this consistently, so the business starts to look forward to them. It's guaranteed to start a conversation, and if anyone ever asks them if they'd recommend a business for what you do, you know who's going to come front of mind.

Contact local groups

There are usually lots of groups that already have your ideal customers attending them. You could contact them and ask to pop along to introduce your business. If you're more confident, you could offer to do a talk on a particular topic that's relevant to them. Sourcing these groups is one job that could be passed on to a virtual assistant.

Partnering with new building sites

New residential building sites usually mean new people are moving to the area. So, offering the sales team an exclusive offer for people moving into their homes is a great way to get in front of people who may not have heard of you yet.

Partner with local schools

Schools have large concentrations of people. You could partner with the school to offer free talks for children and parents. Another way to further show your support for the local schools is to help out at local fayres. Again, make the most of the opportunity with your own brand clothing, lots of promotional material, and a competition to gather everyone's details.

Partner with local colleges and universities

They have access to large numbers of staff and families. Try and get a slot where you can get to stand in front of them and tell them about your amazing business. It's far better to do this face to face with the decision makers and then arrange to present your setting, either via a live face to face presentation, or a pre-recorded webinar that they can watch at their convenience. You may struggle to get the college or university to exclusively work with you promoting your programs, but you could offer the principal or dean a partnership; for every new customer generated, you offer one of their students a work placement in exchange. The leadership board will be happy with this if they see that their learners are securing a work placement opportunity with each referred customer.

Align with a charity

Having a greater purpose and a story behind your business plays a key role in attracting new customers, building loyalty, and ultimately helping change the world. You can arrange fundraising events, get the local press involved, and really help make a difference to a local cause.

Interchangeable text sign

We are constantly bombarded by advertising messages everywhere we go, so we end up becoming oblivious to the adverts around us (we become ad blind). So, if you're in a location where the same people pass your signage every day, they're not going to pay attention to it if it stays the same day in day out. Using an interchangeable text sign allows you to mix your message up. You could come up with all sorts of lines to keep your message original and quirky. Your sign will stand out from the competition.

Press releases

This is a great way to share good news stories with your community and get some free publicity at the same time. The local media are always looking for good news stories that they can share, so take advantage of this great opportunity.

Start by searching online for the contact details for each newspaper. Put them in an Excel file so that every time you've got a new press release you can send it straight to that list, then set a goal on your marketing calendar to submit one new press release every two months. Remember to invite the press along to take photos of any extraordinary events that you're doing.

What Makes You Unique?

Introduction

It isn't enough these days to just be good; customers expect that as the norm. They want to know what separates you from the competition, what unique benefits you provide for them, and why they should spend their money with you over your competitor. So, in this chapter, we're going to be looking at ways to make you unique and set you apart.

Membership discounts

The majority of us like to receive discounts, so why not create a membership card for your loyal customers? This could be discounts for your products and services, or for local business partners. We've had clients get some great discounts for their customers simply by approaching those businesses and explaining what they are trying to do. One of our clients has even negotiated 20% off for all their customers with Costa Coffee. Try and think about what other companies your customers use and if you don't know, ask them. The idea is these companies will form part of your Dream 100 list and you approach them to give you some sort of discount for you promoting their services to your customers. You could promote them on a TV screen in your reception and through your partner brochure. You then give your customers a VIP membership card and a list of all the discounted companies that you work with. Your joint venture partners will get more business, they'll promote you to potential customers, and your customers will get some great savings in return and feel valued.

Promote recent investments

If you've spent money on new equipment, resources, or training, then let everyone know about it. Explain what the benefits are for them. Help your customers see that they're getting more value for their money. It might be obvious to us, but sometimes we need to spell it out to help people truly appreciate the investment. You could do this via photos or video and post it on all of your social media channels.

Your unique mechanism

This is a similar principle to your USP (your unique selling point), but in this instance, what is it about your product or service that gives the customer the result? It could be a new ingredient or process. Not every product or service has one but it's worth spending some time thinking about it.

Features versus benefits

One of the key things we need to get right is the difference between features and benefits. A feature is a factual statement about the product or service being advertised. A benefit answers the customers' question, "What's in it for me?" So, I would encourage you to think about the things you point out to your customers about your product or service. Do you just explain the feature? Be sure to include the benefit for them.

Write your own book

You are already a professional in your area, but writing your own book helps position you as an expert in your field and separates you from the competition. It's a great unique feature that you can promote at every opportunity, through press articles, speaking at local events, and in interviews. You could focus on a particular aspect of your product or service. It needs to be something that people are interested in and want to find a solution for. You don't necessarily have to write the whole book yourself, you can hire a ghost writer to do it with you. Once you've got your book you can give it away to all your potential prospects.

If you'd like to find out more about positioning yourself as the local expert, get a free copy of *Expert Secrets*:

bit.ly/expert-secrets-booklink

Know, like, and trust

Introduction

Competition is fiercer than ever, but in addition to that, horror stories of bad products and services travel fast due to social media. So it's crucial that we start to build a relationship with a prospect, so they start to know, like, and trust us.

Video testimonials

Video testimonials are my favourite type of testimonial by far. There's nothing better than watching a customer tell a story of how your product or service has changed their life. Prospects watching these videos not only see a great example of social proof, but they can often relate to the points customers raise in the video. The customer video may talk about a particular pain point that they had prior to using your product or service, and how that pain point has now gone away.

You can use them on your website, YouTube channel, videos sent out to prospects, social media platforms, and you can upload them as a video to create a social media ad. A couple of tips for you - If you're holding any type of event where customers are coming along, this is the best time to get a number of reviews filmed in one go. I remember an event where my wife and I were at a graduation recently and my wife lined up nine parents in the space of 20 minutes to give us nine new video testimonials. Wine and dine your customers and give them a great experience and they'll happily give you a great review. Another tip is to line up some questions that you'd ideally like them to answer. This way you can make sure you cover off all the fears or concerns a new prospect might have.

Written testimonials wherever you can

The more testimonials you can get the better. Now my personal preference is raw videos, but of course, you can't put videos on printed material, and not everyone wants to watch videos. So written testimonials are great on any form of written marketing material. Here are just a few examples of where you can use them: On your website, flyers, brochures, vehicles, social media platforms, and in email signatures. It's important to include the person's name, location, and a photo. This just provides more credibility that you haven't just written them yourself.

Keep your social proof up-to-date

We've mentioned earlier what others say about you (social proof) is far stronger than what you say about yourself, but this can also act against you if they aren't kept up-to-date. If you have great reviews on your website, but they are all two years old, that's going to leave your customer wondering what's happened to your business over the last two years. So, aim to get at least one new testimonial a week.

Just imagine, if you got one a week, you'd have 52 new testimonials by the end of the year. Google and other search engines prefer it when you've got a steady flow of reviews rather than upload a pile of them at once, so spread them out throughout the year.

Professional video

I remember the first day we put our new video out to the public back in 2014. The impact it had on our business was just amazing. Prior to launching the video, we spent a whole day planning it and arranging for parents to be onsite for the filming. The video cost us roughly £/$5,000 to get produced by a professional videographer. Now you may think that was a lot (and you can actually get your video filmed a lot cheaper these days), but within the first three months of launching the video, we secured over £/$52,000 worth of new business from the video (based on the average yearly value of a customer). That £/$5,000 investment has gone on to help generate over £/$540,000 in new sales (where customers have directly attributed the video to one of the main reasons why they enrolled). So, clearly video is key, as it immediately helps prospects take a look around your setting and see why other customers recommend you. Now video is one of the very first things I produce with my inner circle clients as we can get it produced quickly and start using it on our websites and in Facebook video ads.

Professional photographs

I know a lot of people don't like having their photo taken, but people like doing business with people. So rather than search your phone for a good photo, I strongly recommend getting some professional photos taken of you and any team members. They don't cost a lot if you shop around.

While you're at it, don't just go for the standard headshot, get some fun shots of you laughing and joking around. You'll never know when you'll want to use them in any of your marketing.

Blogging

These days we're all bombarded with emails and sales calls, so it's no wonder why people are more reluctant than ever to give out their contact information. We need to work a lot harder to get that information, and the best way to do that is by providing lots and lots of value. A great way to do this is through blog articles specifically related to your target audience.

Not only does it help you build a relationship with the prospect, but it can also help boost your search engine rankings if done correctly.

It's important to start by thinking of what information your prospects want. This might be a problem they want solving. The great thing is you don't have to write them all yourself. You could hire someone to write them for you or get your team members to help out by recording their areas of expertise and then transferring them into a blog article.

Lead Magnets

Introduction

People are less willing now, more than ever, to give out their contact information, because they are constantly being bombarded with phone calls, emails, and information overload. The old days of simply having a form to opt in for a newsletter are long gone. So, this is where things like lead magnets come in. Lead magnets are reports, PDFs and checklists; documents where people can get access to information that they want to solve a problem, in exchange for their email address.

Let me give you some examples:

- 15 ways to _____ without having to _____
- Top 10 checklist on what to look for in _____
- How to avoid _____ without _____

You're helping the prospect solve part of a problem, but you're asking for their email in return. That way you can start to communicate with them and develop a relationship with them over time by putting them on an automated email campaign. Now online businesses have been using lead magnets for a long time, but a lot of traditional bricks and mortar businesses aren't using any type of lead magnet on their website or in other forms of marketing. So that's a big opportunity for you to take advantage of. In this section we're going to be taking a look at the different types of lead magnets and how you can use them to attract more customers into your business.

Video courses

These have become very popular but are rarely used in bricks and mortar businesses. It's a great way for people to get to know you in a short amount of time. You could do a short series of videos on a number of topics: Your story and introduction, why your product or service delivers the best results, tours around your business, and meeting members of your team. These would be free, but you could create a short, paid course covering your specific subject that could help the customer. They're easy to record on your phone and can be delivered in a number of ways as a short course through Vimeo, or an online portal. You could even use them as part of a Facebook ad campaign.

Email courses

This is similar to the video course, but the idea is that you automate the course through your CRM provider. You can breakdown the topic into small daily email lessons, so people can absorb the content in bite-size chunks.

Active Campaign is a great way to do this. To get a free 14-day trial of Active Campaign click the link below:

bit.ly/cmi-active-campaign

eBooks

eBooks are a great way of adding more value to your audience by helping them solve a specific problem. The idea is that it helps to solve that specific part of the issue. You wouldn't look to cover all of those topics. Focus specifically on one and break it down into simple to follow steps with text and images.

Guides

This topic is quite vast, because there are so many potential topics you could cover specific to your niche, but the idea is you provide a simple step by step guide on that particular topic, so be as specific as possible.

Send to current lists

It's important to offer your lead magnets to your existing lists. You may have had someone enquire six months ago that was just browsing their options at the time and is now ready to make their decision. You may have a former customer who knows someone who could really benefit from that guide you produced. Staying in contact and providing them with value is key and it's free because it's all done through email.

Free plus shipping

This is a great way to provide something of value for free, but then the customer just covers the shipping cost. This could be a physical copy of your book that you give for free and you ask the customer to handle a small shipping fee. The customer knows they are getting great value and the benefit to you:

- The customer has given you their contact details
- They've made a payment transaction with you

This has already helped you get the customer's trust by opening their wallet to you. Now future transactions can be easier, so long as you provided real value in that book.

It's the same principle as giving away a PDF report or checklist, but you're making a sale to acquire a new lead and getting their address at the same time, so you can add in some promotional information about your business.

This doesn't just apply to books, it could be a printed PDF guide, or video series USB. It's totally up to you to test, but make sure you provide value and over deliver; otherwise you may never get that customer to open their wallet again.

I've included an example diagram below of what a free plus shipping funnel looks like.

TWO STEP - FREE PLUS SHIPPING

If you'd like to find out more about how you can do this with Funnels, then you can get a 14-day free trial to ClickFunnels by clicking the link below.

bit.ly/cmi-14day-trial

Email Marketing

Introduction

Email may not be as popular as it used to be, but it's still an essential component of any marketing strategy. Your email lists are so important because it is valuable data that you own and control. Unlike social media where increasing costs, accounts get banned, and algorithms change, this is data you can communicate with for free and send a specific message to, depending on the list they are in (current customers, old customers, enquiries). Yes, open rates have dropped considerably, so you need to grab attention quickly and stand out from the crowd.

Email forms part of traffic you own and control. Let me explain what I mean. There are 3 types of traffic:

1. **Traffic you don't control** – Random people landing on your website or sales funnel.

2. **Traffic you control** - Paying for ads on places like Facebook as you guide them to your sales funnel.

3. **Traffic you own** – People who have signed up to your mailing lists or bought products from you previously.

Never underestimate the value in marketing to your own lists.

Automated campaigns

One of the biggest missed opportunities I see in most bricks and mortar businesses is not having an automated campaign once someone has made an enquiry. So, if someone downloads a free checklist or guide from your website, you've now got their email and can start to communicate with them with the goal of gradually encouraging them to book an appointment. You can share testimonials, USPs, all sorts of information over a period of time, starting with a subtle hint to book an appointment and then making that message clearer as time goes on. Personally, our automations start asking them to book an appointment in the 2nd email.

Follow up automation campaigns

The automation doesn't need to stop there. If you didn't manage to get that prospect to buy there and then, you can then kick off another campaign with the goal of building a relationship with them to eventually get them to sign up or buy.

Here's an example:

If you are a Chiropractor and a patient sees an ad on Facebook promoting a free PDF on dealing with back pain. They may download that free PDF. The first automation will be encouraging them to come in for a consultation. During that consultation you may recommend a care plan. If the customer doesn't sign up there and then, you may add them to another sequence which shares success stories and helpful tips with them, with the goal to them coming back to sign up for the care plan or an alternative offer.

Again, make sure you are sharing more valuable content on why they should choose your business and asking them to fill out a survey of what they thought of your business when they first came in.

Use welcome emails

Even though you'll be calling customers and welcoming them to your business, providing them with an automated welcome email can be extremely helpful to the customer. You can include all sorts of essential information, like what to bring for their first appointment, or reminders for them to like your Facebook page and add you to their safe email sender list.

Include emoticons in your subject lines

At the time of writing this book, 95% of businesses are still using bland subject lines. Including an emoticon in your subject line will ensure your email stands out from the crowd. That additional colour will immediately grab attention and help improve the chances of your email being opened.

Eye-catching subject lines

If you use the same old boring subject lines as everyone else, your email is just going to get lost in the crowd. You need an eye-catching headline to help it stand out from the rest. Things like: "Bad news, I'm sorry, did we do something wrong?" The email that gets the highest open rate on our first automation (driving someone to book an appointment), is the very last email.

Change your email signature

You'd be surprised how many businesses don't have a basic email signature let alone adding these extra elements.

Be sure to include your logo, social media links, and any current campaigns or promotions that you've got running. Keep mixing it up every few months. Your email signature is a perfect opportunity to get increased sales if you make the most of it.

Create a regular newsletter

A printed newsletter is always better than an email newsletter because it's something physical that you hold and can mail to customers, but if you don't have the capacity for that, you should at least be sending an email newsletter. It's a great way of regularly keeping customers and prospects up to date with what's going on in your business. Be sure to include valuable content, such as useful articles, a staff interview, and ways to use your product or service, anything that your customers can get great value from. Yes, some self-promotion is ok, but keep this to a minimum.

Include P.S. notes

Have you noticed how you always tend to read the P.S. note at the bottom of emails and letters? It's because it always stands out away from the main text, so make the most of it. It's a great place to repeat the core message or call to action of the email.

Gather new customers' challenges

It's important to ask every new customer what their biggest challenge was when looking for your product or service. Not everyone will reply, but overtime you'll get a clearer picture of exactly what challenges they had and why they chose your business. You'll be surprised at some of the answers but knowing this additional information will allow you to amend your marketing accordingly.

Automation

One of the hardest things for small business owners is to remember to follow up with customers who have enquired but have not yet made a purchase. One of the huge benefits to using a system like Active Campaign is that it will not only build a relationship with the customer through email, but will also allow you to schedule tasks and follow up reminders with the prospect. No more searching for the emails or follow-ups that you did, this system allows you to keep it all in one place.

Active Campaign is a great way to do this. To get a free 14-day trial of Active Campaign click the link below:

bit.ly/cmi-active-campaign

Event Ideas

Introduction

Events are a great way to build a relationship with your existing customers and provide the perfect opportunity to invite prospects along to get a feel for your business. In this section we will look at the events you can run along with the opportunities your local community provide to get your business out there.

Attending charity events with customers

Popping along to a local charity event with one of your customers to show your support is a great way for building relationships and showing you care about the local community. You could offer to support the charity as your nominated charity for the month.

Community seminars / workshops

A great way to bring your target audience together is by putting on seminars and workshops for them to attend. Ideally you want to do it in your business if you have the space, so they get to see your wonderful facilities, but holding them at a local venue still allows you to develop that relationship with the prospect. Why not run a poll on Facebook to your existing audience to find out what events or courses they would be interested in and then invite your prospects and existing customers to bring a friend?

Customer appreciation events

Put on a big fancy party for all of your existing customers to thank them for being part of your business. Invite any partners you have along to give them a chance to meet your customers. Also invite any new prospects along so they can see exactly how you look after your customers. Host awards and get your local partners to sponsor them. You could even raise money for your local charity. Make it a big annual thing that everyone looks forward to.

Social events for customers

There are lots of opportunities throughout the year to invite your customers along. Customer socials, or family gatherings in the park, family trips, Halloween or Christmas parties. Encourage them to dress in fancy dress and then run competitions. Again, it's a perfect opportunity to invite any new prospects along.

Local community events

School fayres, charity events, church events - they all have an opportunity for you to showcase your services and show that you support the local community. Be sure to take along any exciting equipment. Try and get one of your brand ambassadors to come along with you too. Be sure to host a competition inviting everyone to take part and like your Facebook page where you'll be announcing the winner.

Public speaking events

You may not be too keen on the idea of public speaking, but it can have a massive impact on your business if you can gain the confidence to stand up in front of others and talk about your business and share your expert knowledge. There are lots of groups for this, but one of the most universal is a group called toast masters that helps you develop those public speaking skills with others who are also looking to gain confidence in public speaking. I'd really encourage you to find a local group near you and give it a try.

Want more help with your marketing?

If you'd like to find out how to implement these ideas into your business head on over to www.creations.marketing to check out our range of coaching programs.

Pricing & Packaging

Introduction

I've spoken to lots of businesses over the last few years who are worried that their competitors are charging less than them, and I say the same thing to all of them: It doesn't matter that you're charging more than the competition, as long as you can justify the price with a higher quality, unique service. The key thing to point out is there is no point trying to be the cheapest because as soon as someone else comes along and lowers their price, you're forced to do the same, and your profit margin suffers. You want to be in a position where your business is doing really well, and you can continue to raise your prices due to all the unique benefits you offer your customers. In this section, we look at ways to present your pricing and create offers rather than discounts.

Time sensitive offers

Everyone likes to think they are getting a great deal, but that doesn't mean that you need to discount your prices. Constructing an offer, is thinking, *what additional value can I provide to improve the perceived value of my package and encourage the customer to take action now?* For example, you may include a promotional offer - sign up in the next week and get a goodie bag worth £/$97 and access to our online training platform worth £/$297, but you only charge them £/$89 on top of their main fee. The goodie bag and online training platform may have only cost you £/$10, but the perceived value to the customer was far greater, so the customer thinks they are getting a great deal and you get to pocket the extra margin.

Bundle your offer

We all like to feel we've had a good deal. I'm not talking about providing a discount here, as this just devalues your service. What I'm talking about is bundling things together to create an offer. Including other products or services as part of a package that is cheaper than buying them separately has been proven to increase sales (and of course increases your average customer spend). It's important to make it clear that the customer is saving money by buying these things together, so the perceived value is a lot higher. It also reduces the number of options the customer has to choose from, making the buying decision simpler.

Don't be the cheapest

I remember Dan Kennedy (a famous marketer) once saying, "there's no strategic value in being the second cheapest in your market, and if you're the cheapest your competition may just keep trying to undercut you." Now you don't want to be the cheapest, so be confident in your pricing and position yourself towards the higher end and justify to your prospects that not only do you provide the highest quality product or service, but you've also got several unique benefits over the competition.

Reframe pricing

Breakdown the cost into daily or weekly equivalents to help the customer get over their initial impression that something is expensive. Try to put it into context and compare it to something they can relate to. For example, if you are charging for an additional add on product you could say, "That's less than a cup of coffee in Starbucks." Putting it in the contest of other comparable daily expenditures can make it seem much more affordable.

Free has no value

If something is free, it instantly can appear to have no value. Remember, it also needs to have a call to action - go here, call this number to find out more, or to secure this offer. This also relates to promotional offers as well. You could have the most amazing freebie in the world, but it will be perceived as having no value if it's free. Always give something a value. If it's an offer, it helps when it's something tangible that they need to bring in with them like a printed voucher. Putting an expiry date on it also enhances the perceived value and gives people a deadline to take action.

Present three pricing options

When you offer three pricing options, it has been proven that the majority will go for at least the middle option. If you are only offering one price, the customer only has once choice. This also comes back to the 80:20 rule. 20% of your customers will be prepared to pay a higher price for a better product. Of course, the core product you offer won't be different, but a great way to do this is by having offers where you include additional items as mentioned above.

Price guide

Having a professionally laid out pricing guide that is easy to understand is essential. The last thing you want is for your prospect to be confused. Show your pricing guide to others before you publish it to make sure they understand and don't have any questions. Remember to show additional pricing options if you're confident you can show the value.

Visual cues

I'm sure you've seen pricing tables with visual cues like, 'best value', 'best seller', 'most recommended'. These cues (visual or verbal) help guide the customer to your preferred products and prevent them from having to think too much.

Highlight your added value

Usually your customer will try and compare your price against your competition. This is why it is so important to point out the added value you are providing. It's important to show this added value and this is another reason why it's so important to know your competition, their prices, and the services they provide. It's so important to point out what separates you from them.

Offer upsells

Once a customer has made a purchase with you it is much easier to encourage them to spend more. Therefore, what additional products or services could you offer to compliment what the customer has already purchased? I've included an example diagram below which you may have seen online. Once the customer has made the initial purchase they can either purchase more of the same product, or they can purchase a supplementary product or service in addition what they have already purchased.

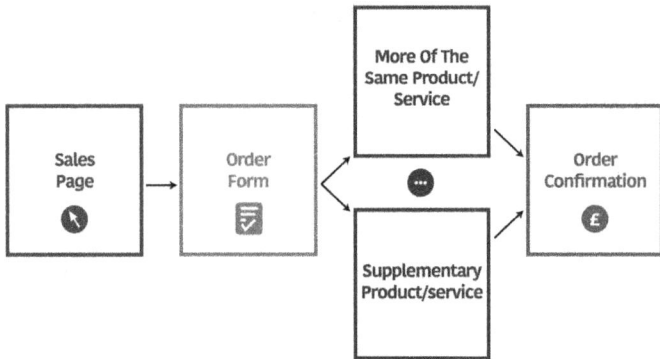

If you'd like to find out more about how you can use sales funnels in your business:

Step 1 – Head on over to Click Funnels to get a free 14-day trial of their software:

bit.ly/cmi-14day-trial

Step 2 – Head on over to our website where you'll find a range of coaching programs that show you how to implement these in your business:

www.creations.marketing

Personal Development

Introduction

This book is packed full of helpful tips to market your local business, but none of them are useful unless you have the right mindset to implement them. Here are a couple of ways to help stay on track to grow a successful business.

Define success

How do you know if any of your marketing activity has been successful if you haven't defined success? It might be the number of enquiries you get, or how many people turn up for an appointment. You can't achieve a goal unless you already have a goal in place. Remember, this doesn't just apply to marketing. How else do you define success in other areas of your business and then share that with your team members?

Keep learning

The same basic principles of marketing that applied fifty years ago still apply to this day, but the way we continue to use those basic principles is constantly evolving. For example, pattern interrupt has always been an effective marketing principle to make your ad stand-out from the competition. When video first came out as an option on Facebook ads, people were used to seeing images and then all of a sudden, video ads started appearing and causing a pattern interrupt. These days, video marketing is common in most sectors, so people are now trying new ways to cause this same pattern interrupt. It's important to keep applying the basic principles but staying up to date with the latest breakthrough techniques in applying those principles is crucial.

Targets in place

If you've got nothing to aim for, you probably won't achieve a great deal. You and your team need to know what the target is for the month and year to ensure everyone is staying on target and is incentivised to do so.

Implement to completion

This book is packed full of ways to market your local business, but without implementation, the advice is useless. I'd encourage you to tackle them one at a time and make sure you've fully implemented the task before moving on to the next one.

Attend events

I know we all lead very busy lives, but I cannot encourage you enough to take time away from your business and attend events. I used to be guilty of always making excuses that I was too busy to go, but I'd always be so grateful when I did go. Not only would

I learn something new, but it would give me time to reflect on my businesses and not be stuck in the day to day running of it. I go back with a clear head of things I need to change or improve, and it always gives me the inspiration to get back to taking my businesses to the next level.

Surround yourself with likeminded people

They say you become the average of the five people you most associate with. So if you're not interacting with other industry professionals, or successful business people that you aspire to be like, then you're not going to develop. It's so important to interact with others you aspire to be like, so they continue to inspire you to reach your own goals.

Accountability is key

One of the benefits of being your own boss is that you don't have to report to anyone, but that can also be a huge downside to running your own business. If you haven't got anyone to hold you accountable, it's too easy to let goals and deadlines slip. I would encourage everyone at all levels of business to have some sort of accountability partner or mentor outside of your family and friends. Someone you know will help set your goals and hold you accountable to achieve them and work with you if you have a challenge with your business.

Would you like help with your marketing?

If you'd like to find out how to implement these ideas into your business head on over to www.creations.marketing to check out our range of coaching programs. and 'done for you' services.

Conclusion

Thank you for taking the time to read this book. Right now, you're probably excited at the great opportunities to start marketing your business, but I'm sure you may also be a little overwhelmed with all the information. That's actually a good thing, as your brain has already started working out how you can implement these strategies into your business.

You should feel proud of yourself for sticking with this book right to the end. There's a lot of information that can make a big difference to your business, but only if you implement it. So my advice to you is start right back at the beginning, where we discussed the fundamentals. It's so important to get these in place so you've got a solid foundation before you start spending any money on marketing.

This book isn't something you should just read once and go on with your business as usual. It's an implementation guide that you should keep handy and keep ticking each strategy off as you implement it in your business.

Once the first strategy is fully in place, then move onto the next one and just keep going. The good news is that most of the strategies in the fundamentals section don't take that long to put in place, so you should be able to get through them quickly. Then, it's up to you which strategies you choose from there, as it depends on what you've already got in place. Perhaps you know you'd like to improve your social media, or you may feel that your competition is doing a great job with their direct mail, so start there. Each section in the book will deliver you results, so just get implementing.

Next Steps

I'd love for us to continue to build on our relationship together, so I'd like to present you with the opportunity to join our One Customer Away Coaching program. You can find out more by visiting:

bit.ly/onecustomerawaycoaching

If you already know the basics of marketing and you're looking for advanced coaching or a 'done for you' service, head on over to our website where you'll find a range of coaching programs and more information on our 'done for you' marketing services.

www.creations.marketing

Testimonials

I've been working with Nick across our three nurseries for nearly a year now, and it's been fantastic. He's really made a difference to our business. He makes everybody feel very comfortable. He knows the ins and outs. He's a business owner himself, so he knows the good, the bad, and the ugly about what can happen. He's really pulled our business into the 21st century. That would be the best way to describe him. And he's just great to work with. I can't praise him enough.

So we've really taken a lot of his advice, with regards to new websites, the behind-the-scenes campaigns. We're working through that and we've still got more things that we still want to roll out with Nick. And I brought my team today to his latest training day because I think it's really important for them to actually see what his vision is and what my vision is for the business. It's a big leap, there's a lot to do, but with Nick's steadying guidance, it's been really worthwhile and I think it would be a really good return on investment.

Catriona Savage – My First Friends

Nick has showed us how we can target and market our businesses to get new customers and new clients, and rather just thinking about those clients that you want now and start planning for the future.

I've learnt that had I had this training from Nick a couple of years ago, I'd have probably grown the business that I had previously further than it's gone. I'm starting out now new, with a new business, and concentrating more on childcare. We use Facebook ads, I've realized now that I was doing generic targeting, that I can target specific things, that having an all singing, all dancing website that costs you a lot of money, you don't need that. You can look at funnels and sorting your website and targeting your audience and calling them to an action. Often, I've put leaflets out with, "Come and do this, come and do that", but I haven't called them to an action, and I've realised that's why I've had no referrals or no feedback.

His experiences of looking at the Disney model, just brings it all to the forefront and makes you realise that something as simple as Facebook marketing or working your website in a different way can bring you in so many more clients. You have to remember that at the end of the day, the customer is the most important thing, and if we're not rewarding that person or getting them to get us referrals, how do we expect our business to succeed?

Jo Haydon – 4 Community Trust

I'd heard about Nick from a few other nursery owners, and I was quite intrigued. I haven't been working my nursery as much this year, and I realized that our numbers were dropping. I think it was because I'm the person who normally does all the marketing. So I decided that I needed to get somebody to come and do it for me. I needed an expert to come sort it out for me, so I could delegate it, because I'm busy doing so much stuff. I know what to do with the marketing, I know how to do it, I think. But, I just, I don't have the time to do it myself.

So I turned to Nick. A few people had said that he really knew his stuff. So I came to his event and I was really impressed. I thought, "Yep, he understands what it's like to be a business owner. He understands my challenges. He understands what it is that we're looking for." One of the things I really do like about Nick is that he's not a fake man in a suit. He's a real person who has gone through the issues of running a business.

If somebody's thinking about coming to one of these days, I would say that if you want to learn how to keep your business sustainable, like a loan that's developing as you're taking it to the next level, you're going to pick up a lot of tips. You're going to get lots of ideas, and really simple things that you can implement straight away that will help you to get those customers coming in.

One of the things that has impressed me about Nick is that he doesn't make marketing feel sleazy. So it just feels that it's a perfectly normal part of our business, that we should be encouraging. I don't feel like he's trying to make me rip anybody off, or he's trying to make me be underhand. It's all about actually just delivering what people need, and doing it in a way that suits them.

Okay, so somebody's thinking about coming to one of these events, I would definitely say, "Do it." Take a day out to do it. I think it's great to have the time away from your business, to actually think about your business, rather than just being stuck in the day-to-day, with your phone ringing, with the door knocking, with staff needing attention. It's nice to be able to come away and think about your goals, and what you want your business to be, because you're an entrepreneur, you're a business person.

Roopam Carrol – Beeston Nursery

What attracted me to working with Nick back in January this year was there were a lot of things that I knew we needed to be doing that we weren't doing. Tracking, enquiries, tracking the enquiries that we were converting into customers. And we've really been able to cover all of that and a massive amount more.

So, the way Nick's helped me implement those things in the business is he's actually come along and taken that role off me, and worked with my managers, so they're the ones doing the work, and not me. I was concerned that they were going to think this is just another job that I need to fit into my busy day, but in fact they've absolutely loved it, and the feedback from them was that they actually said they just loved it. They loved the fact that they've got a process to follow, we all know what that process is. He just has a way with people that puts them at ease, and they're fantastic.

So, anyone that's thinking of working with Nick, I wouldn't hesitate to recommend him. It's been fantastic for my business. As I said, we started back in January, and we had a program for 12 months. And I'm looking to continue that into next year and beyond, I'm not looking to stop that program.

Angela Harper – Little Cherubs

I'm the owner of two businesses and initially I thought I wouldn't need to come here. My wife convinced me, and my manager who's been following Nick and they convinced me. I thought, what is this going to be all about? Now, I came here and I've seen him, and he's the real deal. He knows his stuff.

He's actually convinced me to look at areas which I haven't been looking at, because marketing has always been my kind of forte, I thought, until I've come here and he's told me about areas that I'm missing.

That's crucial, especially the fact when he says the amount of money you're actually losing by not implementing these strategies in place. Yeah, I'm in with this. Nick Williams is the real deal. When you're running a business or you're managing a business, sometimes you can get overwhelmed with the amount of work there is, and you can lose your focus on aspects like marketing.

But he covers everything, right from the beginning. But just by taking one piece of information and implementing that, could just change your business completely, especially when he says how much money you're losing.

I'm a quite hard person to sell to because naturally, I would say that I'm a salesperson, so I know all the techniques, and I've studied different things. But when someone's real and someone knows their stuff, you just see it. That's how I became an advocate for it, here now. Before I wasn't, I was driving up, and I was thinking, really, one whole day I'm wasting? Now I'm thinking, jeez, I wish I had done this earlier.

Ajit Sidhu – Serial Entrepreneur

www.ingramcontent.com/pod-product-compliance
Lightning Source LLC
Chambersburg PA
CBHW071722210326
41597CB00017B/2561